Hugging, Hitting and Other Family Matters

Hugging, Hitting and Other Family Matters

Children Talk About Their Families

Compiled by
Naomi Hample **&** Illustrated by
Stuart Hample

The Dial Press New York

Published by
The Dial Press
1 Dag Hammarskjold Plaza
New York, New York 10017

Manufactured in the United States of America

First printing

Library of Congress Cataloging in Publication Data

Main entry under title:

Hugging, hitting and other family matters.

1. Family. 2. Children's writings. I. Hample,
Stuart. II. Hample, Naomi.
HQ734.H9165   301.42   79-10722
ISBN 0-8037-3844-7

To my family, which has
sustained and nurtured me
from the beginning so that I
may, in turn, sustain and
nurture my children

N.C.H.

and to Helen Hample,
who knows about families,

S.H.

Introduction

These reports on families have been selected from over two hundred and fifty interviews with children in the first to seventh grades at the Walden School and the Rodeph Sholom Day School, New York City; Commack Public Schools, Commack, Long Island; and the Murray Avenue School, Larchmont, New York.

Having no training, equipment, or scholarly credentials, our child investigators are able to make their observations on a purely emotional level, and of course they pull no punches to spare delicate feelings.

These ingenuous little reporters do not speak of the dynamics of sibling placement; they talk about the specific brothers and sisters and mothers and fathers they know from experience in the field. And they zero in instantly on what is wrong, or right, about their families.

A simply observed detail (". . . my dog . . . is the only one in the family who is nice to me . . .") reveals the overall group dynamic in one swift, lethal stroke. Underneath that plain observation we sense the basis of the familial relationships that play an integral part in the development of the child.

Some of their reports are funny, some poignant; others are bittersweet—some are biting. But generally, each specimen is judged on a scale that has only two indices: nice —and rotten.

Naomi C. Hample

Hugging, Hitting
and Other Family Matters

Why We Need Families

If there were no families
there wouldn't be no kids.

Bill

we need families to
be taken care of.
to be loved by,
to get breckfast.
and dress you.
to put you to bed.

and all that.
and thats parents.

brian

If we had no families
we would have no brothers
or sisters and mothers
and fathers. and also dogs.

Jo Ellen

I would not like to be
all alone or not be
healthy. This world
really needs familys
so much. I feel sorry
for the children who
are not cared for and
have no familys.

Donna

familys love me
and help me and
they are for me.
thats why we
need familys

sharon

We need families
because you can't
be alone. except for
grown ups.

Suzy

What Families are For

Families are for loving,
for being together,
for sharing many things,

For sharing secrets,
For sharing things we own,
but families are really
for sharing love.

David H.

If there were
no familys
no one could
be born.
Timothy

We need families because
it's nice to be with somebody.

Kathleen

We need families to take care of you and give you food. Unless you have your own money - then you don't need families.

Benja

a family has many uses.
money, food, shelter and companionship.
then there are the members! the father
spends most of his time at the office.
He comes home and usually turns
strict and gives his pay to mother,
shes the maid, chofer, cook and
accountent of the house. Now we
reach the older brother, there are two
types of them. Nice-and mean. I'm
fortunate to have a nice one, Hughie
He beats me up but never means it.
He also leads an incredible social
life. finally we come to younger
brothers. There are also two types of
us. Good- and terrible. I try to
be good and I do a good job.
I stand everything including my
brother. We all fit togeather like
the pieces of 4 different puzzles
but we make it work.

David F.

We need families
because otherwise
we would have
no place to
go.

James

If no one had a
family no one
would live in the
world but God.

Kenny

We need families because if you were sick or got hurt, there would be nobody to take care of you, and they give us clothes, food, shelter and love. If there were no families, it would be very lonely, and quiet and I wouldn't want to live. I like my family because they all take care of me and love me. I don't really hate anything about my family. I hardly ever get punished but when I was little, I used to talk back to my mother, and I had to stay in my room for an hour, or not watch T.V. one night. When I get very angry I yell, only outside.

Mitch

Sisters and Brothers

The best thing about having sisters is you have someone to play a game with or hit.

Danny

The worst thing about
having sisters in
teen is your
always their slave.
Kelly

One day my little brother decided to feed the fish. So he took a plate, a knife, a spoon and a fork. Then he took the fish out of the tank. Then he called me and said the fish wouldn't eat. I told my mother and she spanked his behind.

Josh

My sister thinks she's God,
She always goes around singing
and it drives me crazy.

Martha

I don't like it when my brother kicks me out of his room so he can make his dumb phone calls

Orin

What is the worst thing
about having sisters?
I'm in the middle and my
big sister bosses me

around, and my little
sister always cries.
So you can't win.

Lori

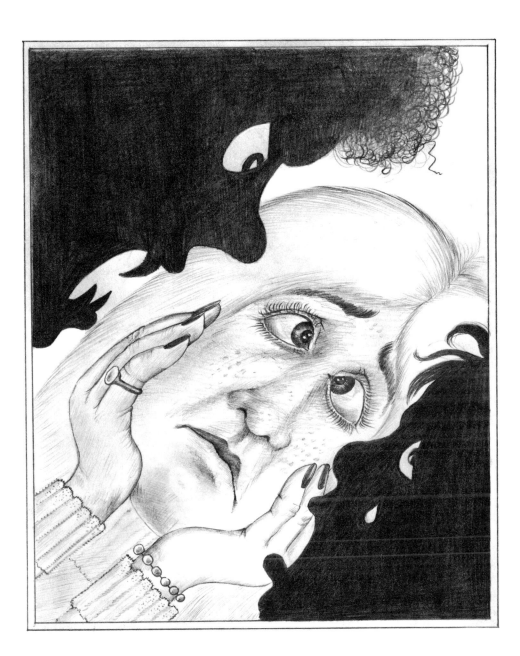

The worst thing about having brothers and sisters is they always hog up the T.V. also they hog up our whole couch and I have to sit on the floor.

Leonard

One day my little
Brother had to feed
the ginie pigs and He
put the hole Bag
of food in the cage.

what a dope.

Ollie

.

When you are the littlest
you get killed. and this is
what it sounds like-ouch-oo
ouch-O O, help mom, ugh
boom bang   your lucky
if your the biggest.

David

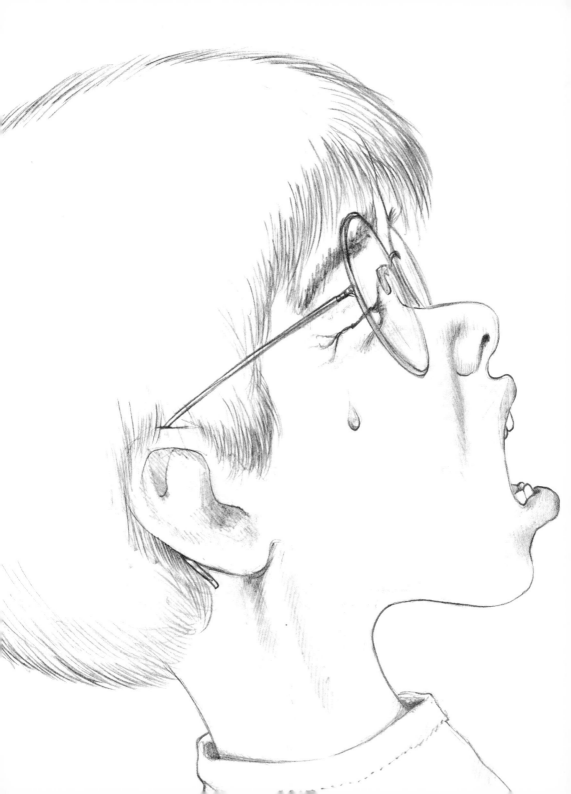

My sister and I use
to always fight.
But for some reason
with a little understanding
on both of our parts we got
closer together. And I though
we would never fight again.

But we did of course be caus
it is imposible to not fight
when you are living with some
one.

Logan

I get punished for punching my sister,

Roberto

My Mother
Sister and my
to school with
leave the house

Wendy

always tells my
Brother to walk
me but when we
they run ahead.

I hate it when my brother teases me, and my mother comes in and says "you _two_ stop fighting!"

Sarah

If I had my choice, I would like either an older sister, or a twin sister to share my feelings with. I don't think I'd like another brother because one is _definitely_ enough

Liz

Fathers and Mothers

The funniest thing
is when my Mother
and father kiss.

Kristen

I'm glad I have a
mother and also a
father because it's
scary when it gets
Dark.

Dina

When I grow up and my children ask me why they can't stay up later, I will never tell them " because I said so. "

Erica

My parents are just right.

They punish their children when they are bad and love them when they are good. They let their children go places but worry about them. I think that's pretty good.

Hilary

I hate it
when I can't
decide what to
wear and my
mother picks
it out for me.

Patrick

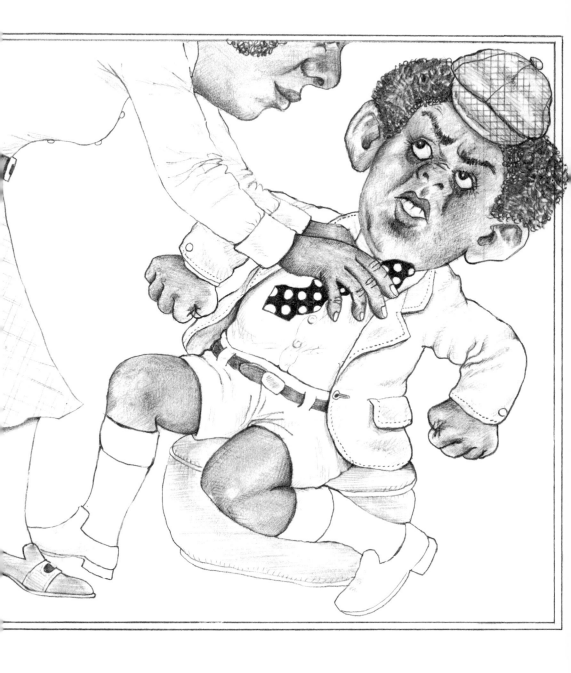

Haiku

I love my parents
Even if they get angry
There still my parents.

Kate

I wish about my family that my mother will stop smoking. A grown up should know better.

Joel

If I had no family the world would be like a large ball in the universe with no meaning. In a family you have to be able to cope with different problems and different people. The point of a family is to have people who you can talk to about problems.

In my family I'm lucky to have such a great mother, father and brother. We have our differences but we talk about them. My father and mother are both doctors and have to give lectures at other places quite often. However they make sure one of them is home at all times. My brother and I get along well, even though I get mad at him and he gets mad at me a lot, we manage. I am grateful particulary for a great family and I wish all people had a family like nine.

ISAAC

I like when my father tells me
stories at night. I don't like
when he tries to make up jokes.
I also don't like when he eats off
my plate when I'm not finished
with dinner. But mostly he's a
nice father.

Julie

When my father
pays bills he says
"OH OH WOW everything
is very expensive."

Denis

I hate when my room is
all messy, and I know where
everything is, than my mom
comes in and cleans
everything up.

My family is almost never together. My parents are seperated. My Mother is with us from Wendsday to Saturday and my father from Sunday to Wendsday. I don't know how they made the schedule which I'm not very crazy about but I know they both love me which is terrific.
                    Linda

One thing I like about having parents is that I always have someone to go to and talk about my problems.

Like once someone did something that I knew was wrong and I asked my mother if I should tell or not. She told me that if I thought I would be helping her if I told OK. And if not it would be best to mind my own business.

Parents are good for solving problems like that.

Anonymous

What I Like best
about my family is
that my mother and
father don't treat me like
a baby anymore.

Carla

MOTHERS

1. ARE made of LOVE & KiNdNeSS & HAPPiNESS.

2. when Your SiCK she Cares for You.

3. when Your SAD she Cheers you UP!

4. when you have PROBLEM You can't solve You Can turn to HER to HELP you.

WHen you come home TIRED & HUNGRY mothers will allways be there at the rescue!

Jo

There are quite a few things I would do different as a parent. First of all I wouldn't meddle in my kids affairs. Also I would keep my sense of humor when my kids fight. And I wouldn't be so protective with them. But my view might change with real kids.

David

I wish my
Parents woudn't
scold me for not
a good reason.
Sam

General Family Matters

Families are sometimes pains.
Your brother bugs you
all day and won't
keep his mouth shut.
My sister screams at you if
you look at her wrong.
Last is your baby brother.
He is cute and playful
sometimes but often he is
a pain. It stinks to be
the middle.   Miriam

families should live in peace

I don't think it's right for all

families to fight. Every time I

go to bed I think very hard

inside my head about my faults

I did today. I don't think

families should fight!

Adam

I Like my family Because They make me laugh

Kyra

I AM THE YOUNGEST IN MY FAMILY. I DON'T LIKE IT. I HOPE MY MOM HAS A BABY SO I WILL HAVE SOMEBODY TO BOSS AROUND.

MELINDA

I wish that my hole family was eight years old

Ralph

I wouldn't want a perfect family. Sometimes you need to get mad at each other and let your anger out. It wouldn't be very nice to be perfect.

Kate

I hate takeing out the garbage. I hate my brother and I hate English.

Anthony

In my family
we have mice
in the basement.

Kim

When I get angry I
storm into the room
and hit my sister
and my LITTLE brother
and yell and scream,
run into my room
and start to hit my
walls and my pillow
and start slamming
the door and opening
it, then I wreck the
room and then I
have to clean it or I
will get in trouble
and then I'm not
angry no more.
Barbara

① What I <u>don't</u> like about my family. My parents are divorsed and my father pays no attention to me and he pays attention to my brother and sisters.

② What I wish about my family. I wish my parents were back together or that my father would pay more attention to me.

③ What is the <u>worst</u> thing about having brothers and sisters are that if I were an only child my father would pay attention to me.

Cindy

If I could change
my family it
would be just me
and my parents
without anybody
else.

Judy

My family is
strange.
thats all.

Julie

The best thing
about my family is
when they fool around
but I like other things
about them to.

Michael

The thing I like best about my family is that I get food. Peter

One   th_ing I love ~~doing~~ doing with my

family is going out to a resTraunt on Satu-

rday or Sunday nigght.

We usually stuff ourself with a good dinner

and then (some) ice cream.x My frather always complains

about the bill, and he always makes us be quiet

or else he will never take us to a Restraunt

again.

But he always f does anyway.

~~SARAH~~

Sarah

What I like
best about my
family? That when
I get picked on
I can Tell because
I'm the youngist.

Nancy

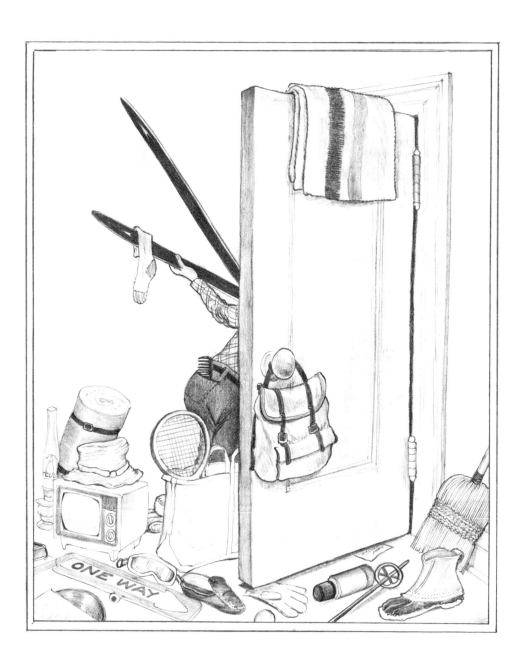

It's a pain when I
have to clean my closet
when I just cleaned
it a month ago.

Jennifer

The Most Unusual thing about my family is that we don't eat any sugar.
Dianne

The thing I like
best about my family
is that whenever there
is a fight we always
make up after.

Josh

I get punished for NOT practising
the piano. If I don't practise
I'm not allowed to do ANYTHIN
It's like a TOURTURE.

Natalie

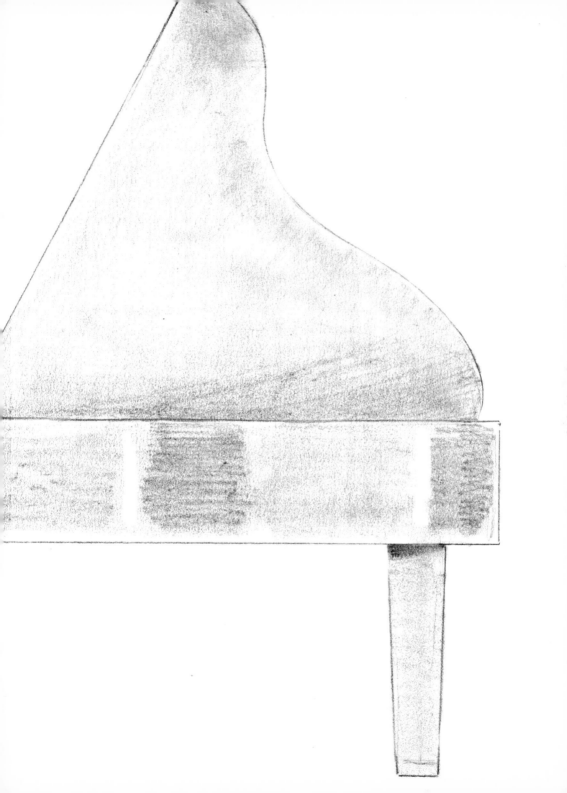

In my family when we
we take a shower they
yell at us that we
use to much hot water.

Elizabeth

If I could have one
wish about my family
I would wish it could
stay exactly as it is.

Nicholas

What I like about my dog. She is the only one in the family who is nice to me.

Cathy

The younger child.
Always refered to as "Rosemary's sister"
    or "John's brother"
Never as Yourself.
For I am my own person
Let me step forward without being in
    this Shawdow.
You will see,
I have my own mind.
I will show you.

Suzanne

When your mad at
Some one in your family,
you can yell at them all
you want.

Mimi

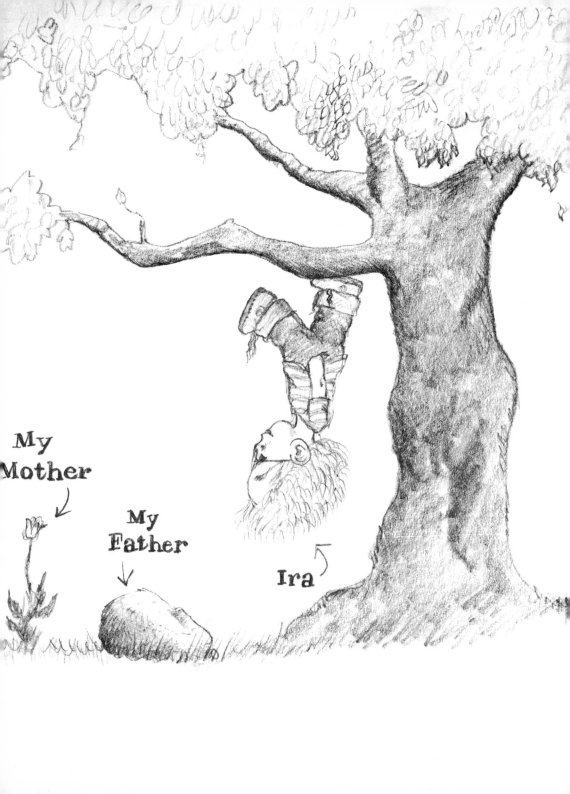

My
Mother

My
Father

Ira

My mother's like a buttercup. My father's like a stone. But I wish Ira could be like a normel brother but he's nutty.

Samantha

the most unusual thing about my family is that we all have brown eyes and so does my dog.

Gina

My family

What I don't like about my family is they always get there own way,

Christine

Families are made up of children, parents and pets. The parents are there to help you when you need them. Sisters and brothers are there to be companions when you need them. Pets are there to play with and cuddle and love. Thats what a family is.

Jessy